SEEKING PEACE
THROUGH RECONCILIATION

MANAGING ANGER AND
RESOLVING CONFLICTS

A GROUP STUDY
PART 1

DONALD E. JONES, PHD

J & A BOOK PUBLISHERS
www.jabookpublishers.com

ISBN-10:1-946368-03-2
ISBN-13:978-1-946368-03-4

DEDICATION

I dedicate this book to my Savior and Lord Jesus Christ. He has been with me every step of my journey upon the Earth, and I so look forward to being in His presence forever and ever.

CONTENTS

ACKNOWLEDGMENTS

I want to thank my wonderful and gracious wife Carol who has supported me in this ministry with sacrifice, enthusiasm, encouragement, and accountability. Most of all, she has been a constant blessing because of her willingness to listen. I was always sharing with her the truths God had been teaching me as I studied His word and wrote this book. It consumed many hours. Thank you, Carol and I deeply love you.

I want to thank my son Gregory R. Jones for volunteering to be the primary editor of this important book. Without his time and effort in painstakingly and meticulously going over every word and every sentence checking and rechecking the sentence structure and grammar, I would not have been able to complete it. Thank you for your ministry to me. I love you my son.

I want to thank my other children, Krista, Matt, and Kara for their love for Christ and His Word and their willingness to live for Him. I love you all.

Introduction

This series of two books (Part 1,2) grew out of a desire to put the material in my main book on seeking peace through reconciliation into a format for group study. As a result, the introductions are exactly the same in both of the books. This is primarily due to the essential nature of the content to aid in our understanding of the truths found in each one. It also allows the books to be read and studied one after the other or to be studied independent of the other one. This provides more flexibility to the various individuals, groups, churches, and organizations who wish to use it.

In Matthew 14, after the feeding of the 5,000, Jesus sent His disciples by boat across the Jordan giving Himself time to disperse the crowd and find a place to pray alone. About the fourth watch of the night (3:00am - 6:00am), the boat was being battered by waves from a strong wind, and Jesus was seen by His disciples walking on the water. At first, they thought it was an apparition and screamed in fear, "It's a ghost!" Then Jesus cried out for them not to be afraid and identified Himself. Then in verse 28-29, the apostle records, "Peter answered him and said, 'Lord, if it is you, command me to come to you on the waters.' He said, 'Come!'"

So, Peter got out of the boat, walked on the water, and headed toward Jesus. Then he looked up and saw the great wind all around him. His eyes turned toward the sea, and he saw the powerful waves. Even in the presence of the Son of God, He became frightened and began to sink. He cried out for Jesus to save him. The Lord responded by immediately stretching out His hand and taking hold of him. Though the Lord could have said many things, he simply asked Peter, You of little faith why do you doubt?" Jesus walked Peter on the water to the safety of the boat. All became calm.

Often, we are like Peter in our relationship with Jesus. We love the Lord, and yet make mistakes, misunderstand His words and actions, and even fail to trust Him. We let the winds and torrents of our lusts and desires to get in the way of our devotion to Him. We allow the stormy seas of trouble and tribulation to make us doubt His intentions and power. We allow the flowing waters and winds of our busy lives to make us treat Jesus as an apparition and not a real person. Yet, regardless of how far we have sunk in our stupidity, weaknesses, and rebellious sin, He always reaches His hand out to restore the relationship we have with Him. The Lord Jesus is always willing to accept our struggles, tolerate our weaknesses, and forgive our sin. He is constantly reaching out to make peace with us. At every turn, Jesus, our Father God, and His Father, and the Spirit are ready to reconcile and restore the conflicts we bring into our relationship with Him.

Here is the point of mentioning this story. God desires the same out of all His children. This is found in several critical passages in the Holy Scriptures. Two of them are mentioned by our Lord and one from the apostle Paul. All three clearly explain the truth that relationships are to be "reconciled" and "restored" to "gain back" our brother, sister, or neighbor. This is done by seeking peace through reconciliation. We should constantly seek to resolve our conflicts with people.

In Matthew 5, the Lord Jesus discusses the heart attitudes people in God's kingdom should possess. After speaking of anger, the Lord presents a general principle of living in His kingdom on Earth. In verses 23-24, He explains, "If therefore you are offering your gift at the altar, and there remember that your brother has anything against you, leave your gift there before the altar, and go your way. First be reconciled to your brother, and then come and offer your gift." The Greek word translated "reconciled" means "to make changes." It originates from a Greek root word that was a banking term meaning "to render accounts the same." There would be a discrepancy between two bank ledgers, and all the mistakes would have to be found and corrected in order for them to agree. We express this between people as "being on the same page." The Lord indicates that the Father desires His people to come to Him fully reconciled with each other. If we, as Christians, know that someone harbors something against us, we are to take the initiative and go to them and reconcile with them. We should not wait for them to come to us. We take our responsibility and go to them. We must once again "settle accounts." They have the same responsibility.

In Matthew 18, Jesus discusses those who are sinning in the church and what all believers should do. In verse 15, the Lord commands, "If your brother sins against you, go, show him his fault between you and him alone. If he listens to you, you have gained back your brother." The Greek word translated "gain" refers "to obtaining or securing something." When a relationship is restored, we gain back everything that the other parties contributed. In this particular case, we have something against our brother, rather than the reverse. If this does happen, we are to take the initiative and confront our brother or sister to gain him or her back and restore the relationship. So, whether someone has something against us, or we have something against someone else, the procedure is essentially the same. Christians must take the initiative and reconcile with them.

The third passage involves the restoration of a sinning brother in the church. In Galatians 6, Paul opens the chapter with an explanation of how to help a sinning saint. In verse one, Paul asserts, "Brothers, even if a man is caught in some fault, you who are spiritual must restore such a one." The Greek word translated "restore" means "to render fit, sound, or complete; to mend or repair what has been broken." The word is used of a physically broken fishing net. In Mark 1:19 and Matthew 4:21, when Jesus called James and John into ministry with Him, they were in the process of "mending" their fishing nets. They were mending the holes in their net so the fish would not fall through. This restoration could easily involve a conflict between two people. Holes in their relationship need to be mended. This process involves the seeking of peace with others. Keep them in mind.

These two books are original works on reconciliation and resolving conflicts. It is not based on other books that I have read and simply collated. To produce this work, I carefully read through the entire New Testament verse by verse and meticulously perused the Old Testament paying particular attention to the Psalms and Proverbs. As I read, categories were built from the individual passages, rather than a set of preconceived notions. These numerous categories became the individual biblical principles found in each chapter. Every passage was studied in its historical, grammatical, and scriptural contexts. Then, I compared all my interpretations with those of past and present scholars. After this study, I have attempted to obey and follow these biblical principles in my own personal life and also utilize them in my pastoral counseling practice. I have seen the Holy Spirit use them to transform relationships of all kinds.

One last thought. At the end of each chapter, I discuss a counseling experience. Due to confidentiality, none of these are based on one particular counseling situation. Instead, I have mixed together common elements I have seen, details from books and films, bits from my own life and the lives of people I have known, and thoughts from my imagination to create a situation where the biblical principles discussed in the chapters can fully be applied. These are composites of real-life situations. Read, learn, and apply.

Chapter 1

Put Away Anger

In a conflict, the biggest hindrance will be our anger. This beast can rear its ugly head during any step in the conflict resolution process. It can and will destroy all the progress we might have made in a matter of minutes using just a few words. Anger is able to build a wall so high that any words or actions to restore the relationship (see Introduction) can't be heard or seen. It can spread like fire to anyone connected to the relationship. These people will usually divide up and create two great armies among family, friends, church members, co-workers, and fellow students for battle: those who take our side and those who take the other's side. The loved ones who remain neutral may be ostracized.

This displeases God the Father (1 Corinthians 1:10; 12:25). We know that God desires peace and unity (1 Thessalonians 5:13; Hebrews 12:14). Anger destroys this peace and unity in our relationships. As a result, this crazed beast of negative emotions and feelings must be managed and its expression in thoughts, words, and deeds must be eliminated. It should never be allowed to reign free and run amuck. It will spit its division producing poisonous venom onto everything and everyone in its path. I use disturbing images because of its disturbing destruction. This incensed monster of anger will shatter real unity within a church, marriage unions, parent-child bonds, friendships, and also disrupt the flow of the gospel from believers to unbelievers.

Often times, anger will actually add to the conflicts we are trying to resolve! If we are able to control our anger, we may even prevent the conflict from occurring in the first place or at least be able to resolve it quickly and efficiently. When all our angry feelings and emotions are managed, then our relationships will remain strong and save us a lot of trouble and difficulties we create for ourselves. If we are also able to prevent the expression of the other person's anger, another mess will not be made. In this chapter, we will learn how to respond to our own anger and the anger of others.

A Typical Scenario

Have you ever had or heard a conversation with a spouse, parent, or friend that went something like this? You might say, "Oh, I am so upset! It's almost family reunion time and this year I wanted to go to the cabin at the lake. For the last three years, everyone else got to pick where we went, and now it's my turn.

Then my younger brother phoned me and described the horrible time he experienced last summer at the cabin with his asthma. Apparently, the altitude is too high and the air too thin for him. He spent the entire week trying to catch his breath. Now he wants to have the reunion near a beach, where he can breathe freely. That is not what I want! So, we got into this big argument! Oh, I am so angry! What a wimp! I am telling you it is all in his head! I'm not bending this time. I want what I want for a change! He better watch out, when I get angry, there is no telling what I might do!"

The person in this scenario let his anger takeover, and evil began just as quickly. This has happened to all of us at one time or another, but it is not God's way. Numerous conflicts that we experience in our relationships are due to or are intensified by our anger. When we get really angry, we want to fight it out with our words and sometimes our fists. This ruins relationships and never builds them up.

A Scriptural Principle

This principle for resolving all conflicts will deal with the techniques needed to put all anger away thereby preventing the sinful thoughts, words, and actions that destroy people's lives. We will discuss how to respond to the anger of others in order to preserve the relationship. This brings us to the first principle which is "we must put away all anger in our relationships." Our natural feelings of anger must always be managed, but their expression in our thoughts, words, and deeds must be eliminated. This is a life-changing distinction. Angry feelings may arise, but they must not be expressed in any angry thoughts, words, or actions. There is absolutely no place in relationships where anger produces positive effects; instead, they are always negative. Though some people may consider "fighting something out" is a good idea, this never works and is not God's way; therefore, this is definitely the wrong way. So how does the Lord desire that we handle our angry feelings when they arise?

A Biblical Explanation

Anger is one of the only emotions that God's children are not allowed to express. This is a bold statement! Allow me to explain. Whenever anger is discussed, our Lord's cleansing of the temple is always brought up. Many believers think because Jesus expressed His anger, the saints may express theirs. They usually cite the cleansing of the temple as proof that the Lord had a righteous anger and simply expressed it. Since Jesus expressed His anger and we are to be just like Him, we may express our anger. The only caveat is that it must be righteous. We can only get angry at things which make God angry. Sometimes, we may have to overturn some tables in people's lives. There is only one problem with this thinking; Jesus did not cleanse the temple in anger.

In John 2:17, after Jesus cleanses the temple the apostle recorded, "His disciples remembered that it was written, 'Zeal for your house will eat me up.'" The Greek word which is translated "zeal" means "intense feeling, passion, and very strong emotion." It does not mean, nor does it imply anger. This is a direct quote from Psalm 69:9, and the Hebrew word is also translated "zeal," not anger. The Lord had so much "fervency in spirit" and "passion" for preserving the holiness and integrity of God's temple that He was compelled to clear out the money changers on two different occasions. This was done from His authority as the Son of God which is why the apostles never did this.

There is one incident that the usual word for anger in the Greek language (not this word) is used of Jesus which can be found in the account of the restoration of a man's withered hand in the temple on the Sabbath. In Mark 3:5, Mark writes that Jesus was angry and sorrowful at their hardened hearts. Neither had been directed at them personally, but instead at their hardened hearts. In Matthew 5:21-24, Jesus condemned anger as murder of the heart as he addressed the true heart intent of the sixth commandment. He explained when anger issues forth into angry thoughts, words, or any actions, these are also sins of "murder," but "murder of the heart."

Paul continues to elucidate God's truth concerning anger. He teaches this principle simply and clearly in two different passages. In Ephesians 4:31, the apostle commands, "Let all bitterness, wrath, anger, outcry, and slander, be put away from you, with all malice." In Colossians 3:8, he then repeats, "But now you also put them all away: anger, wrath, malice, slander, and shameful speaking out of your mouth." Paul commands us to remove all anger and wrath. The first word refers to a general anger and the second refers to the kind of anger that is quick-tempered wrath. Both are condemned by the apostle Paul. He will not allow either.

8

This is taught in the Old Testament as well. In Psalm 37:8, David urges his readers, "Cease from anger, and forsake wrath. Don't fret." Here he uses the three Hebrew terms that designate general anger, quick tempered wrath, and hot rage respectively. Then the inspired writer commands us to cease, forsake, and don't act on them. He explains, "It leads only to evildoing." The inspired writers and our Lord all agree that anger is to be put away when it wells up inside us.

Of course, the question then arises, "What about feelings of anger, are they also sinful?" Sometimes, we feel angry. It comes on suddenly without forethought. One minute we are calm and peaceful, and another minute, we are angry and bitter. How can this be sinful or wrong? Paul answers these two questions in his discussion of anger in Ephesians 4:26-27. He commands, "'Be angry, and don't sin. Don't let the sun go down on your wrath, and don't give place to the devil." The Greek word translated "be angry" is the standard word for general anger.

Let's take a moment for a short Greek grammar lesson. The verb "be angry" is in the present passive imperative tense. It conveys three crucial meanings. First, the verb "be angry" is in the "imperative" which means it is a command. Second, it is present tense which denotes continuous action in present time. This means that the anger does not just arise and leave as fast as it came, it could stay awhile. Third, the verb is in the passive voice which indicates that it has been instigated by an outside source. Something from outside the person is prompting the inward feeling.

The anger is on the inside, but someone or something is provoking or stirring it up whether that is the intention or not. It comes upon a person without their volition. They do not make a conscious decision to get angry, it just happens to them. Their feelings become aroused from within their humanity, and Paul is recognizing the fact that some may become angry without premeditation. Then, a feeling may come upon them suddenly and it stays awhile. It does not come and go. Those feelings of anger are not the sin. Feeling angry is not sinful; it is the manifestation of the feeling of anger in our thoughts, words, and deeds that is sin. This is a critical distinction.

Now the passive voice indicates that it is not brought on by oneself because this would be the middle voice. We can continually stimulate ourselves to anger, but Paul is not speaking of this. Why is this distinction important? Like any emotion, anger can be nurtured within ourselves to grow in intensity and frequency. We can actually enjoy getting angry and lashing out which would instigate us to become angry. We could even practice it. It can become our personal "go to" response when things do not go the way we would like. The feelings of anger that come upon us are not sinful but can become sinful as we nurture and stimulate them. When the angry feeling is stimulated from outside us, it is not sin but can be sinfully expressed. This is why Paul says, "And do not sin." When anger is suddenly aroused, we are tempted by the flesh to express it in our thoughts, words, or deeds. So, believers are commanded not to sin, when they get angry. This means no matter what people do in any of their relationships, they may not express their anger in thoughts, words, or deeds.

In Ephesians 4:26, Paul continues, "Don't let the sun go down on your wrath." This word "wrath" is a different word than the first one. The Greek word translated "wrath" here emphasizes the provoking of the anger. The provocation itself is in view. So, Paul is essentially saying, "Do not let the sun go down on the provocation of that anger." Whatever instigated the anger must be dealt with by sunset. In our vernacular, we would say ASAP (as soon as possible). At the very least, some action must be taken to resolve the issue by sunset. This is the intent of Paul's words. It may take longer than a day, but we should get started. Otherwise, we will be continually provoked and then become angry over and over again. The simplest way is to discuss the issue immediately.

This cannot always happen because we may be unable to let the anger go long enough to really discuss it. So, the next best approach is to set up a time to resolve the issue. The appointment will help calm the situation. So how do we deal with the anger when it comes? Let's begin by thinking of our anger as a ball of fire in our hearts. When Solomon speaks of the problem of pursuing after lust, he uses the analogy of fire. In Proverbs 6:27, Solomon asked, "Can a man scoop fire into his bosom, and his clothes not be scorched?" (DEJ).

Then in Proverbs 29:8, Solomon utilizes the fire analogy for the devastation that one's anger can bring. It sets a city on fire. He explains, "Mockers set a city on fire, but wise men turn away anger" (DEJ). Let us think of our feelings of anger as a ball of fire that may well up in us and could be thrown at others through angry thoughts pouring forth in words, and deeds. Do we nurture those flames, or do we extinguish them? It depends on what we decide to do. We can churn it within our hearts like one makes butter by continuously thinking angry thoughts about the person (Proverbs 30:33). This only makes it bigger and bigger in our minds. We can let the fire within us smolder all night until it explodes into horrendous words and actions from our evil plotting (Hosea 7:6). We can immediately throw that ball of fire at the people who have transgressed us and destroy the relationships we have with them. Or, we can extinguish the flames God's way by "to putting it away" or "putting it off."

In Ephesians 4:31, he uses the first term and in Colossians 3:8, Paul utilizes the second term. Both describe this process.

11

The Greek word translated "put it away" means "to remove it or take it away." The Greek word for "put it off" refers to the "putting off an article of clothing or putting something aside." Here, Christians are commanded to remove it. The flames must be extinguished completely. Though Paul does not really provide the exact process, it would have been very familiar to the Jewish saints from the Old Testament. In fact, Paul alludes to the passage by using the same phrase, "Be angry, but do not sin" (Ephesians 4:26).

This same phrase is found in Psalm 4:4. In this dramatic psalm, David is angry. Many opponents have risen against him, and he cries out to the Lord in prayer. As he describes his anguish, he turns his attention to his future readers and explains what to do when one of the Lord's people is angry. In Psalm 4:4, he writes, "Tremble, and do not sin; meditate upon your bed, and be still. Selah" (DEJ). Here David speaks of trembling in anger because his enemies are spreading lies about him. He is so angry that his whole body is trembling. Have you ever felt that way? We all have. So, sometimes we may get so angry, we begin to tremble. Yet, we are not to sin in thoughts, words, or actions. When this fire has welled up in us to the point of trembling, what do we do with it?

First, we go to our bed. Though this might sound strange with careful consideration, it makes perfect sense. They lived in a Bedouin world of tents. Like our bedrooms of today, the room with the "bed" would be separate from the other rooms by a covering. This would be the only place someone could be alone. He does not mean to literally go to our beds but to remove ourselves from the situation which is provoking the anger. We might call it today taking a "time out." We must leave the scene of the crime, so to speak. Our bed is a quiet spot away from the provocation. It fits perfectly with Paul's injunction to "put it or take it away." We literally take the ball of fiery anger away from the situation to a restful place.

The Hebrew word translated "bed" can also mean "lying down." This word conveys the idea of resting and relaxing.

Second, we should "meditate." This is not the concept of meditation we have today. The Hebrew word literally means "speak or talk." Who are we speaking to? We are talking the situation over with God through prayer and the Word. We are dealing with our anger and battling it inside us. We are recognizing that to express our anger is wrong and will not glorify God and only destroy the relationship. During this time, we should pray for wisdom (James 1:5) and search the Scripture (Psalm 119:50). It is only through these that we can subdue our anger and renew a biblical perspective.

While we are involved in this process, David explains the final step, "be still." Stop everything else. All of our thoughts, words, and actions come to a halt. Our body stops. We stop and take the necessary time to process the situation in our minds. Here too is the sense of relaxing. He is essentially saying, "Calm down." The Hebrew word translated "be still," can also mean "be silent, still, wait." In Psalm 62:1, the Psalmist peacefully utters, "My soul rests in God alone. My salvation is from him." Then in verses 5-6, he writes, "My soul, wait in silence for God alone." This is not the waiting for God to speak in some audible voice, but it is our Lord God preparing our hearts through His Holy Scriptures for reconciliation, not argumentation. Then he adds this, "For my expectation is from him. He alone is my rock and my salvation, my fortress. I will not be shaken."

Then, there is a "Selah" which is like a Hebrew pause in a song. It is as if he is saying, "Please pause, this thought is over. This is the process. Do it! The trembling will cease." So, how can we translate into real life? If our spouse, child, friend, or even acquaintance says or does something which upsets us and we feel the boiling begin to bubble, we need to leave the situation. Then, we should meditate until we are calm and peaceful. The resolution of any problem cannot come in the heat of anger. If we do not get angry but the other party does, then we must take the initiative and tell them we both need a time out. We should never engage their anger. The situation must be defused.

In Proverbs 15:1, Solomon writes, "A gentle answer turns away wrath, but a harsh word stirs up anger." Our angry response may only stir up their anger even more. If believers respond gently, this will turn away any anger. We should respond gently to an angry person. We might say, "I think it's time we took a time out!" Then we must walk away from the angry person. It is critical to make a simple statement and then walk away. If the situation dictates, we ought to repeat ourselves once and then leave the situation. The Lord does not want His people to quarrel.

An Ancient Portrait

From 1 Samuel 13 to 2 Samuel 21, the Bible provides an example of a relationship between two men with opposite reactions to an issue between them. One refused to put away his anger and desired revenge and the other was patient and sought reconciliation. This is the story of Saul and David, the first and second kings of Israel.

The Bible indicates that an evil spirit began to torment Saul. The king's advisers suggested that a righteous man named David come and play the harp to console him and ease the anguish. This was the same David that had just been anointed by Samuel. He knew this, but they did not. In 1 Samuel 16:18, the advisers described David in these words, "Then one of the young men answered, and said, 'Behold, I have seen a son of Jesse the Bethlehemite who is skillful in playing, a mighty man of valor, a man of war, prudent in speech, and a handsome person; and Yahweh is with him.'" He was a man as distinguished as Saul himself, though not yet known by the people.

So, David was called to play music to soothe Saul's pain, whenever he was tormented. At first, Saul loved David and made him his personal armor bearer. So, when Saul went out to battle, he depended on David to carry additional weapons and to protect him if needed. Then one day, a giant named Goliath appeared. You may remember the story of David facing Goliath. David came to the battlefield to feed his brothers and discovered that this arrogant monster of a man was taunting the great armies of the Lord God.

Since the Lord had delivered him on numerous occasions from lions and bears, he would face and defeat this arrogant warrior. With a slingshot and five smooth stones, David killed this mighty giant. It was over quickly in God's power. From that day forward, Saul would not let David go back home. Saul wanted this young warrior in his service right away. Saul's son Jonathon and David became close friends. Saul set David over his entire army, and he won battle after battle. After each of these courageous victories, the women would come outside with tambourines and other musical instruments to celebrate the victory. Now they sang, "Saul has slain his thousands, and David his ten thousands." Saul became very jealous, and his anger was aroused. In 1 Samuel 18:8-9, it is described this way, "Saul was very angry, and this saying displeased him. He said, 'They have ascribed to David ten thousands, and to me they have ascribed only thousands. What can he have more but the kingdom?' Saul watched David from that day forward."

Here is the anger that we have been discussing. Saul and David had a good relationship. Then, Saul's anger literally flipped the relationship from good to bad and soured it. Saul was filled with suspicion, displeasure, and bitterness toward him now. That victory song became a game changer. After this, the relationship with David suddenly became extremely volatile. Subsequently, the evil spirit that was tormenting Saul returned. Rather than David's music calming the king, it upset him. So, Saul grabbed a spear and threw it at David attempting to pin him against the wall. This happened twice, but David was able to escape. Saul did not want to murder David at this point but only to scare and intimidate him.

Before, Saul loved David; now he wanted nothing more than to put fear into his heart. This has happened to all of us. Someone we have a relationship with gets angry and then tries to intimidate us? The "old man" thrives on this anger and intimidation. That is why the old man has to be "put off" (Ephesians 4:22). Since Saul realized David was too well known to simply kill him, he had to devise an alternate plan. Perhaps, he could erase him from the minds and hearts of people by sending him away to the farthest outpost of his army. The people could not forget because David was still winning victory after victory. His reputation grew with each victory. This only made Saul fear him even more. Saul knew in his heart that God was prospering David in everything he did, and the entire nation loved him. This made David a real threat to his throne. Rather than dealing with his anger, he churned it (Proverbs 30:33), and let it smolder (Hosea 7:6), while he devised an evil plan to kill David.

Saul decided to offer his older daughter Merab to him if he would continue battling the Philistines. He was hoping that David would be killed in battle; then, King Saul would look innocent. David refused because he felt unworthy to marry a king's daughter, at least this one. Sometime after, the king discovered that Michal, his daughter, loved David, so he offered her to him. His anger had so blinded him that using his daughters as bargaining chips meant nothing to him. When become blinded by rage, we may not care who gets hurt in the process.

Rather than pay the usual dowry, Saul wanted David to kill one hundred Philistines. The king thought surely the Philistines will finally kill him. Instead, David took a group of men and fought those Philistines and killed two hundred of these deadly enemies. This only made Saul more afraid and fueled his anger toward David. So, David married his daughter, and Saul continually obsessed over him in anger. Eventually, it was all he cared about.

The anger had finally taken over his life. The more David went out to battle, the more victories he won, and the more the people admired him. Now, it became time to get his son and his servants involved in his desire to end David's life. Since Saul knew that his son was David's closest and dearest friend, he demanded that Jonathon and his servants kill David. His anger did not concern itself with the feelings of others, even his own children. Rather than comply with his ridiculous and wicked demand, Jonathon hid his best friend.

After several other incidences, David fled that night. So, Saul sent messengers to watch David's house, so he could put him to death in the morning. When Michal found out, the daughter of Saul quickly let him out through a window to escape. She deceived her father's men by making the bed, so it looked like David was still in it. When the messengers came, she told them he was sick. When Saul found out, he ordered them to bring the sick man to him so he could put him to death. Sometimes anger has no boundaries. The king was willing to put a sick man to death. He had also forced his daughter to decide between him and her husband. When Saul discovered was deceived, it added to his bitterness. Anger leads only to evil and the destruction of relationships.

Now Saul turned the anger he had towards David and directed it to his own son. The King criticized his son and his son's mother. He accused Jonathon of choosing David over him. His son Jonathon did not realize that he was choosing David's future kingdom over the kingdom of their family. He ordered Jonathon to bring David to him so he could murder him. This finally convinced Jonathon his father was determined to kill his best friend. Jonathon now became enraged. Anger and violence often produce more anger and violence in response. Jonathon secretly met with David the next day, then they said their tearful good-byes, and David departed.

While David was on the run from Saul, he wrote several psalms which were prayers and songs of worship to his Lord. As Saul kept raging against David, he was worshiping the Lord God. He did not retaliate. Why not? Saul was the Lord God's anointed king. While Saul was pursuing David, David spared his life on two occasions. Sometime after this, King Saul and his army were defeated by the Philistines, and he and Jonathon were killed in battle. The story tragically ends for Saul with David becoming king in spite of all he had done to stop him.

Notice, King Saul's anger took control and was constantly raging against David. This put in jeopardy his relationships with his son Jonathon and also his daughters. David, on the other hand, practiced amazing self-control. When he was given opportunities to let the full fury of his anger unleash itself on Saul, he refused to take revenge. Why would he not murder Saul for what he had done over and over again? The answer is simple; David thirsted for righteousness (Psalm 63). For us, this righteousness can express itself through the restraining of our lips, taking a time out, meditating, and resting in the Lord if we become angry. This will preserve our relationships and prevent the long road to reconciliation.

A Modern Anecdote

A widowed senior in my church made an appointment to see me so he could talk about something he had done that literally scared him to death. He told me that he could no longer trust himself to do the right thing. It started with a barking dog. This dog barked all day and all night. Because my client was retired, he was home much more than most of his neighbors, including the owner of the dog. At first, he tried to ignore it. Then he put on music to drown out the barking. After this he wore earphones whenever he was home. It wasn't long before he felt he was a captive in his own home. Then he got angry. Anger welled up in him that he had never felt before.

As the days wore on, his anger turned into a deep and dark bitterness for his neighbor and this dog. Why didn't the neighbor do anything? It wasn't long before he was done with it all. He had enough. He tried spraying it with water every time it barked, but the animal seemed to enjoy it. After weeks of this incessant noise, he finally snapped. He began to conceive of a plan to rid himself of this nuisance once and for all. He researched poisons that would kill a dog without detection. He wanted a powder that he could put into a small piece of food that the dog would quickly consume that did not have any real taste or smell. He justified his behavior by telling himself he was representing all the neighbors, and everyone would be glad the barking had stopped.

When the dog was dead, maybe the next one will be quiet and docile. Finally, he mixed the poison into the small piece of ground meat and rolled it into a ball. Then, he waited as his heart pounded for the dog to wake up from his slumber. When the dog did, he flung over the fence. As he positioned himself in a different spot in the yard to get it placed just right, he saw something in his peripheral vision. As the ball of poisoned meat lay there, he went to take a look. When he saw the big furry stray cat sitting on the fence behind his shed, shivers went up his spine. The dog had been barking at that cat! Who knows how long the cat had been there!

He suddenly came to his senses. What in the world was he doing? He turned toward the meat and saw that it was still there. He had not climbed a fence in thirty years, but there he was scaling the fence like he was eleven again. Just as he landed on the backyard lawn, the dog came running. He was so happy to see someone that he hadn't noticed the meat and began jumping up on the man trying desperately to lick his face. The man grabbed the meat and raised his hand into the air. While the poisoned food was out of reach, he saw the dog differently than he had before. Now the man saw the dog as a pet and not a nuisance and annoyance. He found himself petting the animal. The dog calmed down and wagged his tail. When he arrived home, he contacted animal control, borrowed a cage, caught the cat, and turned the stray over to them. The barking stopped. Then he began to worry. How did he ever get to the place where he was about to kill someone's dog? I explained to him the power of the flesh.

When it gets angry, it must be dealt with. Left unchecked, Christians are capable of doing heinous things. We began at the start of the dog's barking and looked at where he had gone wrong. He let his anger dictate what he should do, rather than the principles from God's Word. So, what does God's Word say about this situation? As soon as his anger began to come upon him, he should have taken a time-out to search the Scriptures. He needed to determine not only what to do but how to view this difficult situation from the view of His God. The man would have seen that he did not have a problem with the animal; instead, he had a problem with the neighbor. The Lord God's solution for problems in any and all relationships, whether the relationships are close friends or strangers, is to resolve the conflict with His principles. Instead, the man let his anger control him.

We discussed how important it is to eliminate any anger that might arise for the very reason David gave. If he didn't then it would lead to every kind of "evil doing." He left committed to the fact that the next time he had a problem with his neighbor this senior man would follow carefully the principles of conflict resolution while his anger is in check. Christians must understand the power of anger and how quickly and effortlessly it can take over thoughts, words, and actions.

A Personal Response

Dear Heavenly Father,

I have allowed my anger to get control of me, and it has damaged my relationship with (add name). Please help me to follow the principles concerning anger that I have learned in your Word. Give me the willingness and strength through your Holy Spirit to take the time out needed to prevent any further destruction. I am sorry for what I have done. Please provide the courage I will need to rebuild the relationship with (add name). Then help me to share these principles with (add name) to show him (her) how to deal with me in a holy way when I get angry. I do desire to honor and glorify You in my relationship with (add name). I pray this in the name of Jesus. Amen.

Chapter 2

Cover in Love

Many people feel conflict is inevitable and that arguing and fighting is just a part of life, when this does not have to be the case. The Bible describes three processes that should be engaged in which prevent conflict from ever happening. People in relationships do not have to constantly quarrel and argue whenever conflict occurs. The first process has already been discussed. We should manage our angry feelings and keep them from expressing themselves in angry thoughts, words, or actions. The second and third processes deal with words and actions that instigate the conflicts. Smaller issues should be resolved by covering them over in love. Larger issues should be settled by instituting a biblical decision-making process. In this chapter we will discuss how to cover over the smaller issues in love.

A Typical Scenario

Have you ever had or even heard a conversation between a husband and wife concerning the husband's stepdaughter that went something like this? You hear or say, "Honey, take a look at these craft supplies. They were left all over the table in the kitchen. I have told your daughter many times to pick up after herself. I have a big presentation tomorrow morning and she knows it is the only place in this house to prepare. I have had to take what little time I have and clean up her mess. Guess what? I am going to just throw it into her room. Yeah, I'm going to throw it all over the place, and she will have to clean it up like I did. It will serve her right! (Wife responds.) What? I know she is my stepdaughter and I have been trying very hard to develop a relationship with her. So, you think this will ruin all my efforts with your daughter? (Wife responds.) I don't care, I am really angry! (Husband pauses and contemplates the consequences.) Wait a minute, you are so absolutely right! I can't destroy weeks of building our relationship to see it destroyed over such a small thing. What's wrong with me?"

This man flies into a frenzy about his stepdaughter and then devises a plan to repay her for leaving her stuff out. In his anger, he had chosen to destroy their relationship over a small incident. Then He begins to reflect upon it and realizes it cannot possibly be more important than the preservation of the relationship he has built with her. It certainly will not be worth the long and difficult reconciliation process it will take to restore what has taken him much time to build.

A Scriptural Principle

This scenario illustrates the fact that sometimes important relationships are destroyed over the most insignificant, often ludicrous, and even ridiculous things. In this chapter, we are going to learn how to resolve issues to prevent conflicts in the less important issues of life. Here is an important point: whether an issue producing conflict is important is up to the people in the relationship. If it can be "let go" by both parties, then it should be. If either party cannot let it go for whatever reason, it must be dealt with through the decision-making process. One partner may decide the issue is not important, and the other is being stubborn, stupid, or perhaps selfish. This attitude dismisses and undermines the respect for the other person. Often times, parties in a conflict will dismiss the other person's view because it is not their own. Our view is not just the only view that is important. This deceptive thought will ruin relationships quickly. Principle two is "we must cover over the less important issues in love." Many years ago, Solomon wrote, "Hatred stirs up strife, but love covers all wrongs" (Proverbs 10:12). In 1 Peter 4:8, Peter reiterates this theme when he pens, "And above all things be earnest in your love among yourselves, for love covers a multitude of sins." These two passages which describe the same concept unveil the secret to a very long-lasting relationship. We must allow our love to cover over all the small annoyances, minor irritations, and even the greater transgressions that might occur as we interact in our various relationships.

A Biblical Explanation

In Matthew 5:23, the Lord Jesus stated, "If therefore you are offering your gift at the altar, and there remember that your brother has anything against you." Here He describes a typical believer who is on his way to worship the Father and suddenly remembers a fellow believer has a problem with him. What should he do? In verse 24, Jesus describes the next step, "Leave your gift there before the altar, and go your way. First be reconciled to your brother, and then come and offer your gift." Here the Lord is simply saying that God the Father does not want His children coming to worship Him when a relationship with a brother or sister is not reconciled. If an Earthly father knows that his children are not getting along together, he will address their behavior first before he sees them. Why? He knows that their relationships are very important for the well-being of the whole family. A good father will refuse to pretend that everything is fine when his children are in conflict; instead, he will help them reconcile.

The Greek word translated "reconciled" means "to make changes." It originates from a Greek root word that was a banking term meaning "to render accounts the same." There would be a discrepancy between two bank ledgers, and all the mistakes would have to be found and corrected in order for them to agree. We express this between people as "being on the same page." In our case, both of us have different renderings of the accounts in the books, and I decide that my rendering is not that crucial to the situation. So, I decide to take the other person's rendering. That is the crucial idea. It is important to notice that the verb "reconcile" is in the past tense which indicates the emphasis is on the reconciliation of the other brother with us and not the other way around. We are "to be reconciled," not to reconcile. The emphasis is on what words we need to say and what actions we need to do to reconcile with the person that has the problem with us.

Perhaps, I get into a dispute with my spouse about which route to take to a given event. I consider that getting my way on this dispute is not worth the damage it will cause to my relationship, so I simply decide to go her way. Does it really matter which way we go? Is there truly one right way? A father might be staying with his daughter, and he always forgets his key to her house. Rather than getting upset for the umpteenth time, she covers over this annoyance in love. She might anticipate his weakness and place a key hidden somewhere in the front of the house, so he could find it, if this occurs again. These simple practices prevent conflicts from occurring in the first place.

We learned last time, if the fireball of anger rears its ugly head, we need to excuse ourselves and take a time-out. If the other person gets angry at us, then we should request that he or she take a time out also. We must not engage their anger. We need to take care of the anger first. As we are defusing our anger, we must then decide if the issue is small enough to simply cover over it in love or large enough to engage in a decision-making process. To cover over something in love may be almost instantaneous and require little thought or it may require a serious process. The following are the steps that will help us navigate this important biblical mechanism.

The first step in covering over the smaller things in love is to consider the most insignificant issues briefly and then to overlook them. These are issues that are so miniscule or may occur so infrequently that we can immediately overlook them. They are on such a small scale that they are quickly covered over. In Proverbs 19:11, King Solomon says, "The discretion [good sense, understanding] of a man makes him slow to anger. It is his glory to overlook an offense." He explains that it is to someone's glory to overlook an offense or an annoyance. This essentially means that people bring honor to themselves by overlooking transgressions against them or even the many irritations that bother them.

People demonstrate exactly how honorable they are when they let sins or annoyances go. We cannot possibly confront every person on every word or action that may annoy us. There are simply too many that occur. The Hebrew word which is translated "overlook" means "to pass by" or "to pass through." It is used literally in Genesis 12:6 when God commanded Abraham to enter into the land of Canaan. Moses described Abraham as "passing over or through" the land. In Isaiah 23:2, the word is used of the merchants of Sidon's ships "passing through" the sea.

In our context, it means that we should literally mentally pass by the transgression with its reaction and feelings. We do not allow them to lodge in our mind or heart. We simply move on to thinking about and doing something else. Our minds become preoccupied. This brings honor to ourselves. This is what honorable people do.

The next step in this crucial relationship saving process is to consider some issues more carefully and cover them over in love. These are issues that are simply too big to walk by them but not big enough or important enough to demand a decision-making process. In Proverbs 10:12, Solomon writes, "Hatred stirs up strife, but love covers all wrongs." Solomon explains that when you hate someone it leads only to strife and conflict, but love can help people cover over any and all transgressions or annoyances, if they so choose. The Hebrew word translated "cover" means "to cover over, conceal, or hide."

In Genesis 7:19, the word is used to describe the flood completely covering over the Earth. It is also used of Noah's two sons who walked backward and "covered over" their father Noah's nakedness because Noah had been drunk the night before. They essentially covered over his transgression in their love and respect for him. This is beautiful. They did not use this embarrassing moment as an opportunity to humiliate, gawk, or make a spectacle of him as obviously Ham had done. What a difference? Why do we feel we have to humiliate, gawk, or make a spectacle of someone we love when they make a small transgression against us or annoy us in some way?

In 1 Peter 4:8, Peter draws upon this same principle when he says, "And above all things be earnest in your love among yourselves, for love covers a multitude of sins." Here, he alludes to this very proverb. The corresponding Greek word also translated "cover" means "to hide, veil, and hinder the knowledge of a thing." It was used by Jesus to describe the testimony of believers as a lighted lamp. The Lord told His followers that no one covers over any lighted lamp with a container; instead, he puts it on a lampstand for all to see. In both the Hebrew and Greek, the words also have the idea of hiding it from view or concealing it so no one else can view it. It is more than just not bringing it up, it involves walking backward in respect and covering over something, so the person is not humiliated, gawked at, or becomes a spectacle to anyone around. Is this not a staggering beautiful concept to apply to relationships? Both inspired authors portray this covering process as handling most, if not all sins. Woe to the spouses, parents, children, or friends who "nitpick" every single thing another person does! Why must some scrutinize and analyze every action, as if it is of the utmost importance, then comment, criticize, and humiliate the person?

In 1 Corinthians 13:7, Paul describes love as "bearing all things." The Greek word translated "bear," is a synonym to this same word with an added nuance. It means "to cover, conceal, and hide with endurance." Paul explains that godly love may have to actually endure some transgressions and annoyances of people. We all sin against or annoy the people we love. They do the same to us. A part of that concealing of smaller things is endurance, and endurance is critical to the preservation of relationships. Paul described how he had to cover over, conceal, and bear the weaknesses of the members of the Corinthian church which caused him to have to work to support himself as he ministered to them. In 1 Corinthians 9:12, Paul explains, "If others partake of this right over you, don't we yet more? Nevertheless, we did not use this right, but we bear all things, that we may cause no hindrance to the Good News of Christ."

He gave up his right to earn a living as a preacher of the gospel because he did not want them to think he wanted their money as others had done. He could have demanded financial support from the church and then told them how irritated he was with them as some often do with others. No, he did not; instead, he did not even bring it up, he covered over it in love and went out and worked. He only mentions it in this passage to teach the important biblical truth that they should give up their Christian liberty for others as he did for them. He was always an example.

A similar concept is taught in Ephesians 4:2. Paul exhorts the saints to behave "with all humility and gentleness, with patience, showing tolerance for one another in love." Then in Colossians 3:13, a parallel passage, he encourages Christians to all be "bearing with one another, and forgiving each other, whoever has a complaint against anyone." The Greek word translated "tolerate" and "bear" means "to hold up, to hold one's self erect and firm to sustain, to bear, to endure." The instruction is clear. Believers should "put up with or endure" the annoyances, differences, and even weaknesses of other Christians. The saints must endure and tolerate each other. They should not attempt to humiliate, criticize, and make a spectacle of those Christians who transgress them.

How do we cover over something in love? We reassess our commitment to the person and then decide to cover over the problem because we love them. We ask ourselves this simple question, "Do I love this person?" If the answer comes back in the affirmative, then we decide that this issue is not important enough to even take a chance of destroying even a small portion of what we have together. Then we let it go for the greater good of us both. We simply release the issue. In Psalm 37:8, the psalmist describes this release, "Cease from anger and forsake wrath. Don't fret, it leads to evildoing." He uses a powerful Hebrew word. The word translated "cease" means "to drop and relax." We drop the matter and let the issue go. We decide it is completely over and then relax in our decision.

Then we abandon the issue, walk away from it, and get on with other things. This Hebrew word that is translated "forsake" means "abandon or leave behind." So, we literally walk away from the scene of the "crime" and get on with the business of living. We become too busy with more important issues. In Isaiah 33:15, the prophet Isaiah provides a similar approach to the problem at hand when he says, "He who walks righteously, and speaks blamelessly; He who despises the gain of oppressions." These are people who will not deal with a transgression. They are righteous and will respond to sin righteously. Isaiah continues with this thought, "Who gestures with his hands, refusing to take a bribe, who stops his ears from hearing of blood, and shuts his eyes from looking at evil." These righteous people will refuse the bribe. Then they cover their ears and shut their eyes so that the briber and his bribe are cut off from their senses.

This is excellent advice for our situation as well. We cut off our senses from dwelling on the issue by leaving the area and getting involved with other things. If we need to, we will then relax in the Lord by turning the issue over to Him. In 1 Peter 5:6-7, the apostle Peter encourages us, "Humble yourselves therefore under the mighty hand of God, that he may exalt you in due time; casting all your worries on him, because he cares for you." The Lord God will take care of everything. In Philippians 4:6-7, Paul comments, "In nothing be anxious, but in everything, by prayer and petition with thanksgiving, let your requests be made known to God. And the peace of God, which surpasses all understanding, will guard your hearts and your thoughts in Christ Jesus."

An Ancient Portrait

A beautiful biblical example of covering over the smaller issues in love is the resolving of the issue over land between Abraham and his nephew Lot in Genesis 13. In the previous chapter, God commanded Abraham to go into the land of Canaan. The Lord was giving him and his descendants this land as an inheritance. So, Abraham left Haran, sojourned through Egypt, and landed at the Negev. By this time, he was travelling with his nephew Lot. Both of these two men were very wealthy. They had livestock, tents, possessions, silver, gold, family, servants, and hired men. Unfortunately, they had too many people and possessions to stay together without conflict and had to separate. It became obvious to Abraham that major conflict would arise between them. The number of animals was so large that the men tending them had already begun arguing and fighting over the land to feed them.

So, Abraham took the first step in preventing any conflict. He recognized that they were brothers. This was far more important than arguing and fighting over land, water, and food for their animals. In addition, it would be dangerous to quarrel and become divided. The Canaanites and Perizzites dwelt in the land and posed a real threat to their safety. They would need protection from them. They could not afford to be battling each other over land. So, he affirmed to Lot that he saw them as brothers and did not want conflict between them. He explained that they needed to go their separate ways, so their animals could survive. Then, Abraham did an amazingly unselfish thing. He offered Lot the opportunity to choose where in the entire land he would like to go when they separated. If Lot went to the right, Abraham would go to the left. If Lot went to the left, he would go to the right.

So, Lot took him up on his offer. When Lot saw the valley of the Jordan, he chose that area. Water was everywhere, and it looked like the Garden of Eden. Moses adds that this was where Sodom and Gomorrah were located, before they were destroyed. So, Abraham settled in Canaan and his nephew settled in the valley near Sodom. Unfortunately for Lot, Sodom was an evil, immoral city. Moses calls them "exceedingly wicked." As soon as Lot had departed, God spoke to Abraham and reiterated his promise. God told him to look in every direction, and all that he could see would be owned and occupied by him and his descendants, who would be like the dust of the Earth. So, Abraham dwelt at the Oaks of Mamre. There he built an altar to the Lord God and worshiped Him. Here we have Abraham deciding that his love for his nephew was more important than even the land that he could dwell on. Even though Lot chose the choicest land, his love for him, and the peace between them was a priority. As a result, Abraham prevented a conflict that may have destroyed their close relationship. If he had been upset or angry about the quarreling men, he did not let it become a problem. He was patient and understanding.

Even though Lot had chosen the better land, when Lot was captured by the band of four kings, Abraham and his men rescued him (Genesis 14:1-16). Even though Lot had thought about himself first, Abraham also intervened on his behalf to rescue him from the judgment of the Lord God on Sodom and Gomorrah (Genesis 19:26-33). Abraham could have been angry and bitter over the choice Lot had made and allowed him to be killed by the four kings or the fire and brimstone. Instead, Abraham reassessed his great love for his nephew (brotherly love) decided to cover over the entire problem in love. Then, he released it, relaxed about it, and abandoned it. We need to do the same in our relationships.

A Modern Anecdote

A newly married couple made an appointment with me for counseling. When I came into the lobby, they were sitting on opposite sides of the room refusing to look at each other. I went over to each one and asked them to join me in my office. They walked in one behind the other. The two chairs that they were to sit in were next to each other facing me. Each took a chair and almost in unison moved it two feet away. I asked, "So how long have you two been married?" In complete disgust, they said in perfect harmony, "Six weeks!" I inquired as to who would like to begin this, and the wife responded, "Oh, please let me." She explained that the two of them dated for over a year. The courtship was so romantic, exciting, extravagant, and extremely fun. The wedding was also spectacular and the honeymoon lavish. All was well with their world until they returned from the honeymoon.

They walked into their apartment as a married couple, and he threw his clothes on the bed. She emphasized, "He threw his clothes on the bed!" The wife asked him nicely to pick them up and put them in the hamper. He was fine with that, but he just needed a few minutes to catch the end of the game on the television. He promised he would do it as soon as it was over and flew out of the room. She shouted to him, "But I want it done now!" He mumbled something. She took the clothes and threw them in the bottom of the closet, and they were still there six weeks later. He chimed in that he hadn't needed them. Then he complained that she always forgot to put gas in the car. He could not stand the fact that every time they were on their way somewhere in her car, they had to stop and get gas.

She complained that he was terribly forgetful. He always lost his keys and had called her numerous times to bail him out. She was expected to drop everything and come home to let him in the house. He grumbled that she was always on the phone talking to someone. Whatever they did, wherever they went, the cell phone rang. She whined that he took to many long showers and always wanted the air conditioning on. This was a waste of too much water and electricity. Then her husband moaned about her clumsiness. He had never seen anyone trip and fall, walk into walls, or drop things like she did. This went on for a while longer until things became heated, and then I stepped in. I sat in between the both of them and said, "Since Jesus Christ is here right now and is our Lord and Master, let's see what He might think." They sat silent. Neither had ever considered the possibility that He was actually around and desired their marriage to honor Him. In unison, they asked, "Well, what does he think?"

I explained to them that He wanted their relationship to reflect His relationship with the church. He wanted them to love, nourish, cherish, respect, and understand each other as He did to His church. He absolutely did not want them in constant conflict. Each person brings strengths, weaknesses, and differences to the marriage. Over several sessions, we first looked at the strengths each brought into the marriage and how they could be best utilized. We discussed some of the weaknesses of both partners and which ones could be changed and which ones could not. The ones that could not be changed would be "covered over in love." For ones that could be changed over time, we developed strategies to eliminate them. Then the many differences between them would be taken through a decision-making process and be negotiated. In essence, they should focus on their strengths, cover over the small things, and then negotiate the larger matters. I explained how important it was not to let their anger control their words and actions. The fate of a marriage should not rest on lost keys, an empty gas tank, overuse of utilities, or sheer clumsiness.

A Personal Response

Dear Heavenly Father,

I recognize that my flesh is very strong. I know it is easily annoyed with many of the small things (add name) does. I am so sorry for not loving (add name) in the way that you love me. You are so patient and understanding. You do not hold my salvation over me for every mistake I make. Help me do the same for (add name). I need the wisdom to know when something he/she should be covered over in love. I need the strength and power then to do it. Please assist me in remaining silent and not make a snide remark or subtle jab which undermines the love that I want to demonstrate. Help me to understand that my way is not the only way of doing things. I am so sorry. I commit myself to honoring and glorifying you in my relationship with (add name). I pray this in the name of Jesus. Amen.

Chapter 3

Resolve in Unity

Another way in which we can prevent conflict is to take the larger, more serious issues, problems, and irritations that arise between us to a decision-making process. During this time, we decide how we will handle something together. We should set up some rules and boundaries for a particular situation and follow them whenever the circumstances may warrant. This is critical because it avoids the breakdown of a relationship through a multiplicity of small annoyances and irritations or big blow-ups and intense battles. If we utilize a decision-making process when issues come up, we can avoid many clashes which inevitably will divide us and lead to the destruction of the relationship that often took so long to build. Once a marriage commences, there are often many disagreements over a variety of issues which must be taken to this process as soon as they arise.

A Typical Scenario

Have you ever heard a conversation between a husband and wife that went something like this? He says, "Hi, Honey! I am so glad we are over that fight. I hate it when we fight. It puts this cloud over everything I do. Wow. I'm so relieved. So, I guess since we reconciled, we will buy the new truck after all." (Wife responds.) "What do you mean, you didn't agree to that? We argued over purchasing the truck and then told each other how sorry we were. I thought that meant we would get the truck? (Wife responds.) What! You thought that meant we wouldn't get the truck. Why do things always have to be your way around here? (Wife responds.) What are

37

you talking about? I want it my way. We're done! I'm outta here! You will be lucky if I ever come back!"

The husband in this imaginary scenario thought that each of them telling the other that they were sorry about the argument solved the problem itself. This happens often. We take all the right steps to reconcile with the other person concerning an argument over an issue but actually neglect to resolve the issue itself. We fail to address the problem that started the argument in the first place. We focus on the apology for getting angry and quarreling but never resolve the issue that started it. Then when the situation arises again, and it always does, the argument resumes. We essentially pick up where we left off. Instead, we need to resolve the issue or issues through a careful decision-making process. This is best accomplished before the conflict begins. Since many issues cannot be anticipated, then it has to be dealt with as each one arises.

A Scriptural Principle

This brings us to the next principle. Principle three is "we must decide together on the larger issues in unity." This is how the foundation of relationships is laid. As each issue arises, a decision is made concerning how it will be handled from then on. Both the parties simply have to abide by the decision. This is easier said than done. Both individuals will struggle with adhering to the commitment they have made. They might have to remind each other that they made the decision together and rely on the Holy Spirit to keep them committed. At other times, both parties may decide on one course of action and discover that it will not work, so they return to the decision-making process and proceed through it again. Relationships last for a long time so the parties must put out the effort to make their relationship strong.

A Biblical Explanation

This concept is actually implied in the word Jesus chose to use to describe the restoration process between people in Matthew 5:23-24. You may remember that Jesus declared, "If therefore you are offering your gift at the altar, and there remember that your brother has anything against you, leave your gift there before the altar, and go your way. First be reconciled to your brother, and then come and offer your gift." The Greek word which is translated "reconciled" in the English means "to make changes." The word comes from a Greek root that was a banking term which meant "to render accounts the same." There would be a discrepancy between two bank ledgers, and they would have to find the mistakes and fix them. They must do this until both ledgers match. We express this between people as "being on the same page." For us, we each have different accounts of something that happened between us and they must be rendered the same.

In the last chapter, we decided that our rendering was not that crucial to the situation, so we took the other person's. Yet, there are times we will not be able to do that. We will desire to resolve the books. We must find the error in our thinking, calculations, or even feelings or emotions. It cannot be covered over but must be resolved. For example, we get into a dispute with our spouse about whether to purchase a particular house or not. Perhaps, we argue over whether to discipline our son by grounding him or losing the use of his car for a weekend. These might be too important to cover over. If one of the partners decides that the situation cannot be covered over, then a decision-making process must be set into place, so conflict is avoided.

The biblical decision-making process has ten basic steps. First, we must seek God's will under the Lordship of Christ. We must remember as believers that saints do not serve themselves, they serve the Lord Jesus Christ. When we came to Christ, we confessed Jesus as Lord. In Romans 10:9, Paul defines a Christian in these words, "That if you will confess with your mouth that Jesus is Lord, and believe in your heart that God raised him from the dead, you will be saved." The word that is translated "Lord" means "master, owner, and possessor." We answer to Christ first. In Romans 12:11, Paul characterizes all Christians as those "not lagging in diligence; fervent in spirit; serving the Lord." We should be committed to serving the Lord in all of our relationships, not simply ourselves. As a result, both parties need to seek His will, not theirs. If both people in a relationship are believers, they both should seek God's will. If one is an unbeliever, then the believer should seek God's will in the decision.

This brings us to our second point. Whatever decisions are made, they must be made in unity. As we approach this process, we must seek to preserve the relationship and make a decision in unity. In 1 Corinthians 1:10, Paul describes this principle, "Now I beg you, brothers, through the name of our Lord, Jesus Christ, that you all speak the same thing and that there be no divisions among you, but that you be perfected together in the same mind and in the same judgment." God desires that we find unity in our relationships among the brethren, whether they are our spouses, parents, children, friends, ministry partners, classmates, or co-workers.

Third, we should study the Word and pray. There should be a careful search of the Scriptures for the biblical principles that govern a particular situation. Sometimes, the Lord will speak directly to a situation with a specific principle. For example, He commands that His children should pay their bills (Proverbs 22:7; Romans 13:8). If a couple gets into an argument concerning the expense of a vacation, they should go on the one that they can afford, not the one they cannot. Sometimes, God does not speak directly to an issue, but He will provide governing principles which will guide them in determining His will. Though the Bible does not speak to the selection of specific spouses, it does provide several divine parameters. Here are a few: spouses should be believers (1 Corinthians 7:39; 2 Corinthians 6:14), should love us God's way (1 Corinthians 13:4-8), and should be willing to fulfill their responsibilities as a husband/wife (Ephesians 5:25-33) and father/mother (Ephesians 6:1-4 If the person does not desire these things, then we should not marry him or her.

At times, God provides a general principle for an issue and leaves the specifics up to both parties to decide. An example would be Ephesians 6:4. Paul exhorts all parents to raise their children in the discipline and instruction of the Lord. How they do this is up to them to decide in unity. The only restriction is that they shouldn't exasperate the children in the process. This would involve pushing them too hard, or provoking them to anger, or criticizing them. Another example might be the admonition to serve the brethren or minister to the body (Galatians 5:13; Ephesians 4:12). What ministry we have and how we accomplish it for the Lord is up to us to decide in unity with those involved. Lastly, there are some biblical principles that govern neutral activities which may need some righteous boundaries. Though sports, hobbies, and even artistic endeavors may in of themselves be completely neutral, they can still overstep biblical grounds. Here are several biblical principles which govern these activities. They should not make us think, say, or do impure and unholy things (1 Corinthians 6:19-20), put us in bondage as a habit we cannot remove (1 Corinthians 6:12), tempt us to sin (Romans 13:10), hinder the advance of the gospel (1 Corinthians 10:32-33), dishonor God in some way (Romans 14:23), or weaken us spiritually (1 Corinthians 10:23). When we endeavor to search His Word, we must pray for the wisdom necessary to find these principles, understand how they apply, and for the willingness and power to obey them.

Fourth, we should examine our inner motives. We should be coming to the process to follow the Lord's will, not our own selfish pleasures. We must ask ourselves the question, "Am I concerned about the needs of the others involved or am I seeking my pleasure alone?" In 1 Corinthians 10:24, Paul encourages the believers with these words, "Let no one seek his own, but each one his neighbor's good." The Greek word translated "neighbor" refers to believers or unbelievers in any of our relationships. In 1 Corinthians 13:5, Paul asserts that love "doesn't seek its own way." Our love does not need to seek the betterment of ourselves but all the ones whom we love. It is assumed in Scripture that the most natural instinct is for humans to seek their own good and survival. That's why Paul explains to believers that they are to love their wives as themselves in Ephesians 5:28-33. It is easy to become focused on ourselves and our needs in a relationship, but this is not God's way.

Fifth, we should examine every detail carefully and then suggest various courses of holy action. Paul concludes his first letter to the Thessalonians with a series of injunctions. In 1 Thessalonians 5:21-22, he advises, "Examine all things, and hold firmly to that which is good. Abstain from every form of evil" (DEJ). As we plan a resolution to a problem, we need to take our time. We should systematically examine all the evidence, facts, and issues, not allowing our emotions to cloud our thinking. Then, we can rationally find a spiritual, righteous solution that would honor God. In Proverbs 21:5, Solomon explains, "The plans of the diligent surely lead to profit; and everyone who is hasty surely rushes to poverty." We know this intuitively as evidenced by the old adage, "Haste makes waste."

Sixth, each of the partners in the discussion needs to listen and respond in love, respect, and understanding. This is critical. In James 1:19-20, James commands that the believers should listen before they speak. All parties involved have a contribution to make, and the Lord can speak through all of them when it is according to His Word. In 1 Peter 2:17, Peter sums up how we are to treat each other in this process, "Honor all men. Love the brotherhood. Fear God. Honor the king." We are to show honor, respect, and understanding toward one another. Love, respect, and understanding are the three pillars of marriage or any relationship (Ephesians 5:25; Colossians 3:19; 1 Peter 3:7). Listening will promote understanding, respect will stimulate communication, and love will encourage unity.

Seventh, the parties involved should carefully assess the impact of the solutions which come to mind on everyone who is involved. We find a beautiful example of this in Acts 15, when the apostles with the saints met to discuss whether Gentiles had to become Jews first to be saved. When they considered salvation by faith alone, the answer was no. When they considered the reaction of the Jewish Christians who were newly saved, they asked the Gentiles to consider abstaining from all foods sacrificed to idols, blood, things strangled, and sexual immorality (Acts 15:29). They assessed the impact of the decision to all involved and still followed the Scriptures. The consideration of all involved includes every person affected by our decision: children, parents, relatives, friends, and others. It even involves the yet unborn offspring of future generations. One decision to move to another state away from family and friends will not only affect us now but many generations to come who will not grow up with the family members left behind. The change in an occupation may not only affect us but our spouses and children. If it involves much travel or long hours, we are not the only ones affected.

Eighth, we must be willing to sacrifice and compromise for the good of all. The Christian life is not all about us. The attitude we are to have is summed up in Philippians 2:3-4, "Doing nothing through rivalry or through conceit, but in humility, each counting others better than himself; each of you not just looking to his own things, but each of you also to the things of others." In Ephesians 4:2, Paul adds, "With all lowliness and humility, with patience, bearing with one another in love." In 1 Peter 5:5, the apostle Peter continues, "Likewise, you younger ones, be subject to the elder. Yes, all of you clothe yourselves with humility, to subject yourselves to one another; for 'God resists the proud, but gives grace to the humble.'" All of these truths speak of the compromise and sacrifice which is directed toward others. This must be a part of the decision-making process.

Ninth, wise counsel should be sought, if necessary. Each person individually or together should consult others they trust. In Proverbs 11:14 Solomon writes this, "Where there is no wise guidance, the nation falls, but in the multitude of counselors there is victory." In Proverbs 12:15, he adds, "The way of a fool is right in his own eyes, but he who is wise listens to counsel." In Proverbs 15:22, King Solomon says, "Where there is no counsel, plans fail; but in a multitude of counselors they are established."

Then, in Proverbs 27:9, this wise man urges, "Perfume and incense bring joy to the heart; so, does earnest counsel from a man's friend." Each passage deals with the many positive results of wise counsel. He also describes the many negative results of poor counsel. The "wise" is so important. After his death, His own son became king. The son sought advice from His father's older advisers and his young friends. The elders encouraged Rehoboam to be more lenient on the people than his father. His younger advisors told him to be harsher. He followed the "unwise" counsel of his young advisers, and the people rebelled. As a result, the kingdom of Israel split in two parts and never fully recovered.

Tenth, we should continue the process until we have fully reconciled the issue. All parties must be of the same mind on the solution. This is what Paul encourages the Philippians to do with the issues that faced them. In Philippians 2:1-2, he begs, "If there is therefore any exhortation in Christ, if any consolation of love, if any fellowship of the Spirit, if any tender mercies and compassion, make my joy full, by being like-minded, having the same love, being of one accord, of one mind." In Ephesians 4:3, he asserts that they need to be "eager to keep the unity of the Spirit in the bond of peace." In 1 Corinthians 1:10, he cries out, "Now I beg you, brothers, through the name of our Lord, Jesus Christ, that you all speak the same thing and that there be no divisions among you, but that you be perfected together in the same mind and in the same judgment."

These passages demonstrate the importance of keeping at the decision-making process until the issue is resolved. Once we resolve some of the important issues of conflict in the relationship, it will be much more unified and fulfilling. Many issues in the relationships that I see in counseling are nothing more than a series of conflicts that have never been resolved. They argue over them, then tell each other they are sorry, but never go back and resolve the issues that caused the conflicts in the first place. In our analogy from Matthew five, the accounts are never settled.

An Ancient Portrait

An excellent example of how an issue should be resolved is found in a conflict between two apostles, Peter and Paul found in Galatians 2:11-16. Both were great men of God yet came into conflict with each other. When Paul was on his first missionary journey, he founded the churches in Galatia. They were in Pisidian Antioch (Acts 13;14-50), Iconium (Acts

13:51-14:7), Lystra (Acts 14:8-19), and Derbe (Acts 13:14-14:23). Since he was sent out from the church in Antioch (Acts 13:1-3), the apostle Paul returned and shared all the blessings God had accomplished. Since this occurred mostly among the Gentiles, he was opposed by a group called the Judaizers.

These Jews claimed to be Christians and believed that a Gentile had to become a proselyte Jew first in order to be saved. Gentiles were required to be circumcised, follow all the Jewish ceremonies and dietary restrictions, and obey the Mosaic Law to become true Christians. There was such a contention between Paul and these false teachers that the church sent them to Jerusalem to have the apostles settle the matter. This instigated a meeting of what is known as the Jerusalem Council. This council included all the apostles, James, the half-brother of Jesus, and the church members in that city as well as Paul and Barnabas.

It was decided that the Gentile people did not have to be circumcised or live by the law. They did not have to become Jews first to be saved. The decision weighed heavily on Peter's testimony to the group. Peter had a divine vision in which the Lord explained that He was offering salvation through Christ without becoming a Jew first. The Judaizers refused to follow their mandate and entered the churches of Galatia that Paul established.

These false teachers criticized Paul and were challenging both his ministry and his message. Now some saints were wondering off into false doctrine and denying the person who brought them this gospel. When Peter went to visit the church, he did not follow the dietary laws of the Hebrews any longer and felt the full freedom to eat with the Gentile believers. Why? Eating kosher food only was no longer an issue. Then the Judaizers discovered what Peter was up to!

They pressured the chief apostle until he succumbed and disassociated himself from all the Gentile Christians. When Paul found out, he confronted Peter.

Studying how Paul resisted Peter and how they resolved the issue without destroying their relationship will give us insight into the decision-making process. In Galatians 2:11, Paul describes the encounter, "But when Cephas [actually Peter] came to Antioch, I resisted him to his face, because he stood condemned." Note, there was confrontation face to face. The Greek word translated "resisted" means to oppose or stand against. This does not necessarily refer to an angry confrontation. So, if Paul did get angry, he had already put it away. This word refers to two people who stand against each other in complete disagreement on an issue. Did Paul and Peter argue? No. Paul investigated the situation and discovered who these people were and what they had done.

In Galatians 2:12, Paul determined this, "For before some people came from James, he ate with the Gentiles. But when they came, he drew back and separated himself, fearing those who were of the circumcision." These Judaizers had come from Jerusalem and then claimed they were following James, the Lord's half-brother. They dropped his name for credibility, though James would never have sent them. Peter had eaten with the Gentiles, then drew back and separated himself from them. This Greek word "drew back" has the idea of "shrinking back timidly." Both of the verbs are in the imperfect tense which indicates a gradual separation. Peter slowly separated himself, until someone noticed he was not eating with them anymore. The Gentile Christians thought he was being aloof because they had done something wrong. Has that ever happened to you? You get into a disagreement with people, and they start to stand aloof. They act as if you have the plague, so to speak. They make you feel that you are doing something wrong, when you are not.

47

It became such an issue that many others followed Peter including Barnabas. In Galatians 2:13, Paul describes it, "And the rest of the Jews joined him in his hypocrisy; so that even Barnabas was carried away with their hypocrisy." It is called "hypocrisy" by Paul. So, they knew the truth but were not following it. They were acting like hypocrites. They were not following their own beliefs. Their walk did not match their message nor were they living righteously by separating from the Gentiles. This violated the essence of the gospel.

So, the apostle asked him a question in the presence of all which is found in the second part of verse 14, "I said to Peter before them all, 'If you, being a Jew, live as the Gentiles do, and not as the Jews do, why do you compel the Gentiles to live as the Jews do?'" Wow! Paul knew Peter himself was not living by every standard of the Judaizers. Since he was not following all of their ceremonies or keeping the entire Mosaic Law, how could he attempt to make the Gentiles do it? He was a Jew living like a Gentile and yet he wanted the Gentiles to live like Jews.

Notice, Paul reasoned with Peter by helping him examine his own actions. Then Paul gently corrects Peter. He explains to Peter that as Jews, the law could not save them, only belief in Christ could do that. Once Paul pointed this out, Peter and the other saints repented from their hypocrisy and went back to eating with the Gentile Christians. So, this conflict between these two men did not lead to the destruction of their relationship but a resolution of the problem. So, let us look at the decision-making process and see how this story illustrates it. First, the apostle Paul sought God's will under the Lordship of Christ.

Second, the apostle Paul sought unity with the priority of preserving their relationship. There is no reason to believe that the apostle argued with Peter or even criticized him in any way. Because it was not God's way, it was not Paul's. Third, we can assume he prayed for wisdom and sought the governing biblical principles for the situation. When he confronted Peter, he gave the governing principles that were violated. Fourth, the apostle's motives were not self-seeking or pleasure oriented. If it had been, he would not have said anything at all. Who would want to take on the chief apostle of Jesus Christ? Fifth, he examined everything carefully and then suggested a plan of action: eat again with the Gentiles.

Sixth, we assume as he listened, it was with love, respect, and understanding. There is no indication of the lack of any of these as he speaks to him. Seventh, he assessed how the decision would impact all of those involved. Eighth, though Paul might have compromised if it were another issue, but he couldn't. Why? This was divine truth, and Peter was not following the truth. Ninth, Paul had previously sought the wise advice of the Jerusalem council. Tenth, the apostle would have kept at Peter and the others until they were of the same mind. We can infer that they continued until unity was achieved. We need to follow these holy men as they follow the Lord in using the decision-making process.

A Modern Anecdote

I could hear the shouting from the lobby. My new couple had arrived for their second counseling session. They were so contentious the first session that I had to schedule them after the building had closed and the rest of the tenants were gone. Their conflict revolved around the in-laws. As is often the case, very different people marry and will bring into the relationship very different families. The husband's family was very aristocratic and proper in manners and approach. The wife's family was very down to Earth and did not worry about "appropriate" ways of doing things.

He was an only child, and she was the youngest of seven children. Though they loved their son, the husband's parents were a bit aloof and not used to physical displays of love or words of affection. On the other hand, the wife's parents were all about hugs, kisses, and words of love and devotion. The husband's parents believed that the couple should make all their own decisions and if they needed help, they could ask. The wife's parents believed that the wisdom and advice of every family member (parents and grandparents, brothers and sisters, aunts and uncles, etc.) must be utilized often. It was an insult if a major decision was made without at least consulting them.

Both the husband's parents believed in "having their own space" and not coming over uninvited. On the other hand, the wife's family believed in arriving unannounced. All were welcome at any time. Needless to say, this essentially meant that the wife's family was always around and the husband's was rarely seen. This posed a dilemma for the couple, and it produced a large amount of stress and conflict upon the marriage as each family sought to express their love to the couple in very different ways. The husband resented his in-law's constant interference with their affairs.

The wife resented his unwillingness to accept her family. She loved them, loved being with them, and relied on them for help. She thought his family was cold and unfeeling. The holidays became impossible for him. The husband's family believed that a holiday is celebrated on that day alone. The wife's family believed that every holiday was a week-long event. Just the birthdays alone accounted for nine weeks of the year. How could he possibly keep this schedule up? He would have to get a second job just to purchase the gifts and supplies needed. The relationship began to feel one-sided tipping toward the wife and her family's many expectations. This took several sessions to resolve.

This was my response, "Let's see what the Lord God says about this in His Scriptures." I took them immediately to Genesis 2:24. It reads, "Therefore a man will leave his father and his mother, and will join with his wife, and they will be one flesh." They were now a "brand-new family" unit. The relationships that they both had with their old families had now changed. This is God's plan. When their children grow up, then they will be leaving their old families (them) and then creating a new family. This may be difficult for them to cut the "umbilical cord" and for the parents and other family members to do the same. It will be hard for them as parents when their children move on to their new families, but it is God's blueprint.

As a result, I taught them the process of decision-making discussed previously. Then they made a list of every issue that had to be decided between them concerning how they would now interact with their families and the in-laws. The goal was a decision in unity.

When they had set up their new plan, they were to go as a couple and share with each "old family" individually their "new family" plan. They knew this would not be easy, but they would stay with the plan no matter what the reaction. They committed themselves to prayer and to trust the Lord that all things would work together for their good. As they followed the plan, their conflicts lessoned, and their joy grew.

A Personal Response

Dear Heavenly Father,

I did not realize how many decisions have to be made in a relationship. Give me the wisdom needed to decide whether an issue between me and (add name) is important enough to proceed to the decision-making process according to your Word. Please do not allow me to brush off an issue that (add name) desires to resolve. Help us to find the unity that You have with the Son and the Spirit and so desire for us to have. Give us the willingness and persistence to follow the many principles for decision-making found in Your Word. May we honor and glorify You as we seek true unity together. I pray this in the name of Jesus. Amen.

Chapter 4

Utilize a Mediator

There may be times where we cannot resolve a conflict or reconcile a relationship by ourselves. We may not be able to discern exactly what the conflict is, why it is occurring, or how to find a solution. The problem may be too complex, or it may simply need a fresh set of eyes to view the situation. Perhaps, both of us are desirous of finding a resolution but are too broken, upset, or hurt, to initiate the reconciliation. As these kinds of difficulties occur, it may be time to find a mediator to aid in the reconciliation. This person should take both parties through the process in the Lord.

A Typical Scenario

Have you ever had or perhaps heard a conversation like this concerning a wife and her little sister? She says to her husband, "Wow! Honey! I just finished talking to my sister, and she will not listen to me. I have tried and tried to discuss our falling out, but she will not in any way be reasonable. What? (Husband responds.) Yes, I told her it was partly my fault. I apologized for the harsh and unkind words I said to her at the last holiday celebration. She doesn't want to see me, you, or the kids. Her kids and our kids are like brothers and sisters. How can I possibly explain this to them? They will be so disappointed. I have invested so much time and effort into building our relationship, now it's going to all be thrown away. We are at an impasse. (Husband responds.) What? Really? You think that I should ask my older sister to intervene? (She pauses.) Wait! That's a great idea. She loves us both, respects our older sister, and has always valued her

53

opinion in the past. Okay, I think I will contact her by email tomorrow!" Sometimes, we have a problem with others and finally come to our wit's end in our attempt to reconcile and cannot do it. As in this simple scenario, when this occurs, it is time to seek mediation.

A Scriptural Principle

In Matthew chapters five and eighteen, the Lord Jesus commanded us to reconcile relationships with those who have something against us, or we have something against them. Unfortunately, this cannot always happen. One side may not desire it, or both may not be able to figure out what went wrong or even have the skills to reconcile. When this happens, they will need some help. This brings us to the next important biblical truth. Principle four is "if there is difficulty reconciling, utilize a mediator." These mediators can assist the people involved when they get "stuck" in their problems and cannot resolve them.

A Biblical Explanation

In Galatians 6:1, Paul exhorts the Christians in Galatia to intervene in a sinning brother's life. The apostle explains it in these words, "Brothers, even if a man is caught in some fault, you who are spiritual must restore such a one." He asserts that those who are spiritual should help bring restoration to the brother. Someone else must get involved. We have seen that the "someone" could be the actual transgressor or even the one transgressed, if they turn from their sin and "become spiritual." One of them may have reconciled with God and then goes to the other to help them do the same. Though, in this context, Paul is emphasizing someone else who is doing the work. In our case, it would be a mediator.

This person (mediator) comes alongside someone and helps them repair the net of holes in their relationship with God and then the others involved (see Introduction). The net's holes that were created are too large or too difficult, or perhaps so numerous that the ones involved cannot mend the net themselves. They desperately must find assistance. They must search for a mediator. In the passage, the Greek word for "caught" literally means "to take before." One of two ideas is in view here. One would be a believer sees another believer sinning and he intervenes, before he can hide it. It can also refer to believers who intervene when a sin has overtaken another brother usually by surprise. He is trapped in a transgression and cannot get out of it. This would perfectly describe people who could not resolve their sins against one another.

Therefore, the second meaning fits very well with the case in point. The believers are stuck. The one who is spiritual and desires to restore the relationship (whether transgressor or transgressed) seeks another who is "spiritual" because he cannot mend the net alone. The other person is "caught" in their sins. This could refer to one who desires to restore the relationship but cannot get the other one to budge. Perhaps, some believers are aware of two people not getting along. The two are found caught up in their conflict, and the saints intervene to bring about reconciliation between them. These Christians become mediators that restore the relationship. These very mediators seek to mend the holes in their net.

The apostle discusses this very concept in 1 Corinthians, chapter 6. The Christians in Corinth were suing one another in the law courts before unbelievers and Paul chastises them severely for this. In 1 Corinthians 6:5, he rebukes them and then asks, "I say this to move you to shame. Isn't there even one wise man among you who would be able to decide between his brothers?" Paul demands that believers settle their differences among themselves by finding a mediator in the church. This is what a mediator will do. They will settle the differences and help solve the problem. In Galatians 6:2, Paul states, "Bear one another's burdens, and thereby fulfill the law of Christ." This is the admonition the apostle Paul provides immediately after he exhorts them to restore the sinning brothers. They may need to help them "bear" their burdens. The Greek word translated "bear" here means "to carry off, to carry on oneself." Could this not refer to one carrying on his shoulders the restoration process with the conflicts and sins involved? So, the saints in conflict should seek a mediator if they cannot reconcile a relationship.

Let us begin with the critical qualifications one must have to become a mediator. The first comes from Galatians 6:1, they need to be spiritual. This means they must be a believer and be "filled with the Spirit" when they mediate. In Acts 6:5, when a dispute arose between the Hellenistic Jews and the native Jews in the serving of food, the apostles chose seven men "full of faith and the Holy Spirit." The reason for this is that someone must mediate the dispute exercising the fruits of the Spirit. The second one has just been discussed from Galatians 6:2. One must be willing to bear the burden of the situation. In Acts 3:2, the same word is used to speak of those who had to carry and bear the physical weight of the lame man, so he could gather alms. In Romans 15:1, Paul speaks to those spiritually strong in Christ and says, "Now we who are strong ought to bear the weaknesses of the weak, and not to please ourselves." This requires spiritual strength to carry out the burdens of the weak. People with a weakness in resolving a conflict should pick those who are spiritual and strong (Step 1) and willing to follow this injunction (Step 2) in order to mediate.

The third qualification is wisdom and discernment. They need the kind of wisdom and discernment that is capable of solving the problem in the Lord, not in some worldly way. Remember, Paul commanded the Corinthians to find a wise man among them to settle their disputes (1 Corinthians 6:5). This wisdom would involve a knowledge of the Scriptures. In Psalm 119:24, the inspired writer affirms, "Indeed your statutes are my delight, and my counselors." Later, in Psalm 119:66, he asserts, "Teach me good judgment [discernment] and knowledge, for I believe in your commandments." So, they world but the people of God are not wise old sages spewing forth the wisdom of the speaking forth divine wisdom from the Scriptures. In 2 Timothy 3:16, Paul writes this, "Every Scripture is God-breathed and profitable for teaching, for reproof, for correction, and for instruction in righteousness, that the man of God [saint] may be complete, thoroughly equipped for every good work." The Scriptures can teach, rebuke, correct, and train. They are thorough and complete in their equipping for every good deed. When people are having conflicts, they must know exactly what "good deed" God wants them to do to resolve the issue to find peace with one another. The Bible can do all of that.

The fourth quality is that mediators must be spiritually respected by both parties. This is actually implied in the first and third quality. Would not selecting the wise to mediate according to 1 Corinthians 6 imply someone who would be respected? Does not wisdom produce respect from others? This wisdom would include knowledge, discernment, and respect. When Moses was judging Israel, his father in law observed the toll it was taking on him to resolve all of the disputes among the people. In Exodus 18:21-22, he explains to Moses how to delegate the responsibility. Jethro instructs Moses with these words, "Moreover you shall provide out of all the people able men which fear God: men of truth, hating unjust gain." Would not this produce respect among the people? Do you remember Acts 6? Here men filled with the Spirit and faith (men respected) were appointed to settle the issue between the Hellenistic and native Jewish saints in the Jerusalem church. We are to do the same.

The fifth quality is to find people who can empathize and show compassion for both sides. These mediators must help the two parties in conflict go through a difficult healing and restoration process which requires a tremendous amount of compassion and empathy. In Hebrews 2:16-17, our Lord Jesus Christ is called a sympathetic high priest who comes to our aid in times of trouble. The author expresses it in these words, "For assuredly He does not give help to angels, but He gives help to the descendant of Abraham. Therefore, He had to be made like His brethren in all things, so that He might become a merciful and faithful high priest in things pertaining to God, to make propitiation for the sins of the people. For since He Himself was tempted in that which He has suffered, He is able to come to the aid of those who are tempted." As we can see, like Christ, mediators should be sympathetic as they aid in solving disputes.

The sixth quality is someone who has invested something in the lives of both parties or at least in the one who has the difficulty in reconciling. This way, the mediator can make a personal appeal to one or both of the parties. This was a powerful strategy that Paul often used. In the city of Corinth, Paul had many difficulties in turning them back to God and appealed to the fact that he had brought most of them to Christ. Paul was their spiritual father. In 1 Corinthians 4:15, the apostle reminds them of this, "For though you have ten thousand tutors in Christ, yet not many fathers. For in Christ Jesus, I became your father through the Good News." Before Paul exhorts the Thessalonians to behave in a godly manner, he spends the first three chapters describing how he had ministered among them in sacrifice, service, hardship, and love. Then in 1 Thessalonians 4:1, he states, "Finally then, brothers, we beg and exhort you in the Lord Jesus, that as you received from us how you ought to walk and to please God, that you abound more and more." Then the apostle spends the last chapters speaking about things that needed to be changed in their church which included their sexual immorality, unwillingness to work, false beliefs about the death of the saints, and their lack of appreciation for their leaders. They had unruly people who needed to be rebuked, faint-hearted ones who needed real encouragement, and others who were spiritually weak that needed help. So as can be seen, finding a mediator who can appeal to them in some way out of love, service, or devotion can be extremely helpful.

Once we understand what kind of mediators we need, we must find them. Where can believers find mediators? The first place is in any of the "accountability" groups God has given His people for the protection of relationships. They may find them among immediate or extended members of the family (Proverbs 1:8; 2:1; 3:1, 21; 13:1; 15:5; 19:27; 23:19-24; Psalm 29:17; 71:18; 78:1-5). The parties in conflict may ask the church leadership to intervene (1 Peter 5:2; Hebrews 13:17; Titus 1:5; 1 Peter 5:1-2; Proverbs 11:14). In the church, mediators can be drawn from one's fellowship or ministry groups (Proverbs 27:9; Romans 15:14; 1 Corinthians 4:14; Colossians 1:28; 3:16; 1 Thessalonians 5:14; 2 Thessalonians 3:15). If conflict involves legal issues, then mediators should come from appropriate government agencies as in the case of divorce (Romans 13:4; 1 Peter 2:13-14; 1 Timothy 2:1-4).

Grown children can mediate which would demonstrate much honor and respect toward their parents (Ephesians 6:1-2; Deuteronomy 5:16; Leviticus 19:3). A professional Christian counselor may be able to more skillfully mediate a conflict using principles from the Word (Proverbs 11:14; 12:15; 15:22; 19:20; 20:18). In actuality, any Christian who is spiritual might mediate, especially those with particular gifts geared toward this particular kind of ministry (Ephesians 4:11-12; Romans 15:14).

Once we have found mediators who might qualify, what do they do? They should follow the biblical principles which are outlined in this book. They are to lead both the parties through the steps of reconciliation with God first and then reconciliation with each other. The mediators should become guides and take the parties involved through the entire process. They might decide to meet with each of the parties individually at first. Other times, they may want to meet together. They should basically walk the ones in conflict step by step through the process. In our net mending analogy, they bring the parties together and show them how to mend the holes together.

An Ancient Portrait

A perfect portrait of discipleship is found in the apostle Paul's relationship with Onesimus whom he had brought to Christ. This is found in the letter to Philemon. When Paul arrived in Rome, he met a runaway slave named Onesimus. After Onesimus came to Christ, Paul discovered that his owner was a dear friend of his in the city of Colossae named Philemon. For a time, both Paul and Onesimus ministered together, but it came time to return him to his master so he could face the consequences of his crime. This was a serious offense in that society.

Rather than just let Onesimus return and face it alone, he decided to use the opportunity to teach both Onesimus and Philemon some important truths concerning reconciliation, the true fellowship between followers of Christ, and obeying the law. This was a great discipleship opportunity for the both of them. Paul was the right person to do it, since he was both the spiritual father of Onesimus and Philemon. He was also an apostle of Christ, who was well respected in the church. So, Paul sent a letter on behalf of this new believer which recommended that Philemon reconcile with him and welcome him as a new brother in Christ rather than as a fugitive slave who deserved severe punishment.

The apostle begins his letter complementing Philemon on some qualities, he is now going to have to display with his newly returned slave. He lauds him for his love toward believers and his deep faith in Christ which he now wants him to show toward Onesimus. Then, Paul asserts that as an apostle he could command Philemon to embrace Onesimus but would rather entreat him as someone who loves him in Christ. He could ask him as his spiritual father but would rather entreat him as aged prisoner of the Lord Christ Jesus to make peace with him.

He could appeal to Philemon's commitment to the Lord but would rather implore him as someone who himself has made many sacrifices for the Lord. Philemon needs to do the same in this difficult circumstance. Paul asserts that God really had a purpose in this slave running away, and it was for his salvation. Philemon has Onesimus back as a beloved brother in the flesh and the Lord. He is especially a beloved brother to Paul. Rather than punishing his new brother as a slave, he should be embraced. Then Paul mentions that the slave may have owed him money probably either through theft or through the money lost in his absence of service so he would pay for it. Though Philemon could have afforded it, Paul did not want the loss of his friendship. He speaks of the joy and refreshment of his heart he is going to feel when he learns what Philemon has done.

His joy and refreshment will result from Philemon not only obeying but even going beyond his many suggestions.

Then he indicates that he would be coming for a personal visit, so Philemon would face the apostle himself. This will definitely encourage Philemon to do what was needed to be done. His companions also greeted him.

This will encourage his right actions because they will know of Philemon's treatment of Onesimus also. There were several: Epaphras, Mark, Demas, and Luke. These were his fellow workers and mighty men of faith. Two of these men, Mark and Luke, wrote New Testament gospels. Though we are not told specifically what happened, we can be assured that Philemon welcomed Onesimus into his own household and church at Colossae. There is no indication anywhere in the Bible that Paul had to mediate the situation again.

Perhaps, once Paul's letter was read, Philemon did the unthinkable to the unbelieving Roman world, he unchained and released Onesimus. Then this Roman master, Philemon, reached out his hands and cried, "Welcome, my brother!" Here, the apostle Paul demonstrates, for not only Onesimus and Philemon but all Christians, exactly how a mediator mends the broken net of a relationship between two saints. Once resolved, this conflict should not appear again. If it does, the process may be used again to resolve the conflict.

A Modern Anecdote

There are numerous people who are involved in various kinds of ministries in the church. This can be such a blessed time when we constantly put the Lord Jesus first and desire to humbly serve and glorify Him. Unfortunately, after we come to Christ, we are still human and have a flesh that constantly entices us to desire things our way only, even in ministry. One day, I received a phone call from a pastor who had two Christian ladies in his office who were in charge of the new mom's ministry in the church. They both loved the Lord but were from two different generations with different personalities. The younger one (middle twenties) was a bit of a free spirit, very creative, and a people person. The other one was an older woman (senior years), who had managed various ministries in several churches was serious, focused, always functioned with proper planning, and was more task oriented. The pastor asked the two women to work together.

This would follow Paul's injunction encouraging the older women in the church to teach the younger women. The younger woman was a brand-new mom who made up for her inexperience with great enthusiasm and high energy. The older woman had raised five children, now had twelve grandchildren, and even two great grandchildren. She was experienced and capable but moved slowly and precisely. From the first day in service together, the two women had clashed. The younger woman really wanted to start calling moms about the new ministry, and the older wanted to take some time and design a flyer to put in the bulletin.

The younger woman wanted a simple time of prayer, bible study, and fun. The older woman desired to train the new moms systematically on all aspects of motherhood and child development. The younger woman wanted to have the moms host the weekly meetings in their homes so everyone could be a part. The older woman felt that it should be in the church nursery where it was safe and secure. Every single suggestion one of them made was countered by the other with the almost the suggestion opposite. Then, they came to a standstill.

They were driving each other crazy and had not yet had one meeting with the new moms. The word got out that these two were having so many difficulties that none of the moms wanted to attend because of the conflict. The pastor

MANAGING ANGER AND RESOLVING CONFLICTS

realized that those ladies needed a mediator. They agreed to see me if I would come to his office, and the church could pick up the cost. I asked the pastor if he could sit in on the counseling as we dealt with these two ladies that were having so much difficulty. When I arrived, I had each lady tell me her side of the issue. Once this was provided, which I just described, I explained to them that in every relationship, the parties bring into it many strengths, weaknesses, and differences.

Their strengths need to be embraced and the weaknesses should be eliminated if possible or planned for when not, and the differences must be negotiated. Then I taught them the decision-making process found in this chapter. We made a list of their strengths that they brought and divided up the various tasks according to those strengths and their other abilities and gifts. We discussed some of their weaknesses and created a plan for each supporting the other, if needed. For example, a signal would be used when the younger woman was speaking too long and beginning to go off the planned program during the meeting. Another signal would be given if the older lady became rigid and would not allow something spontaneous to occur. Next, we discussed what they thought was left to be done. This negotiation took time and there was compromise on both sides. Finally, we looked at the biblical principles that concerned unity under Christ's Lordship. We prayed and a new mom ministry was born.

A Personal Response

Dear Heavenly Father,

As I was reading this chapter, it suddenly dawned on me that I really need a mediator to assist me in reconciling my relationship with (add name). Lord, help me to take my full responsibility for everything I did to ruin the relationship with (add name). Open up (add name)'s heart to the biblical principle of utilizing a mediator. Soften our hearts so we both may follow what the mediator recommends as he (she) follows these principles. Guide us in our search for a wise mediator that we can both agree upon and give him (her) the wisdom, understanding, patience, and empathy necessary to mediate. May the three of us honor and glorify You as we restore the relationship. I pray this in the name of Jesus, my Lord. Amen.

Conclusion

As we conclude this book, I would like to leave us with some final thoughts about our God of reconciliation and what His Son did on the cross for us. First, if we understand the full extent of what was wrought for us on that cursed tree in order to make peace with us, it will become so much easier to do the same thing for others. Second, if you read this entire book and realized that you do not understand salvation or have never received Christ as Lord and Savior, then I would like to provide that opportunity. Please do not skip this section; it may be the most important in your life.

From all outward appearances, humans seem "good" and attempt to live decent lives. This is man's concept of himself. This is not God's concept. The Almighty's view is that people all over the world and throughout the ages sin, sin, and sin again (Romans 3:23). This is a terrible and utterly destructive condition. Yet, they have ramifications that are far worse. These sins condemn us to everlasting divine retribution.

Though described briefly in the Old Testament, the Lord Jesus Christ clearly announced and proclaimed the future punishment to come. Contrary to popular belief, Jesus did not only speak of love, grace, and mercy, He also spoke of the coming judgment for sin. He declared that the judgment of sin would be everlasting punishment in a place He called "Hell." The Lord portrayed this place as an eternal inferno (Matthew 18:8) where there would be the weeping (from the sorrow) and gnashing of teeth (from the agony and anguish of suffering) continually into eternity (Matthew 8:12; 13:42, 50; 22:13; 24:51; 25:30; Luke 13:28).

Why must people face this horrific punishment? Though God is a God of love, grace, and mercy, He is also a God of great holiness, righteousness, and justice (Psalm 89:14,18). These attributes are just as much a part of His divine nature as His love, grace, and mercy. You have broken God's law as we all have, and the penalty must be paid. This began with the first man Adam (Genesis 3:1-7). When this occurred, His love, grace, and mercy surfaced, and a provision was made. Someone else would have to take man's place and pay the penalty. Someone who had never transgressed Him, who would never deserve punishment, and would fulfill all of God's Laws, would be substituted in man's place. This was the Son of God, Jesus Christ.

As the God-Man, He would pay the penalty for our sins in His death on the cross. Once done, the Lord God made only one provision for people to appropriate what His Son had done on the cross for them. This provision is receiving Jesus Christ as Savior and Lord. Though I cannot possibly share with you this good news in the confines of this book, I would love for you to consider purchasing my book entitled, *Finding the Light: The Kingdom of Heaven and How to Enter It*. It can be found for sale on Amazon.com. It is inexpensive and contains the full gospel message for your consideration. This message is so important and extensive that it cannot adequately be contained in a few pages at the end of a book.

If you are a believer, you must go out into the world and seek peace through reconciliation as God did for us. These principles are to be lived and shared with others. You now have the tools to make your relationships last a lifetime. Go live them out and share them with others!

ABOUT THE AUTHOR

Dr. Donald Jones is currently a Christian Pastoral Counselor with thirty-eight years of experience in the fields of pastoral ministry, public education, and Christian counseling. He carries degrees and certificates from four major universities and from a variety of educational institutions. He has been a professor of Languages and Bible, a television commentator, and a featured speaker at a variety of events and seminars at churches, schools, and other organizations across the United States. He is a member in good standing of several secular and Christian professional organizations. Dr. Jones has been a published author since 1976. For further information view his website at www.donjonesphd.com.

www.ingramcontent.com/pod-product-compliance
Lightning Source LLC
Chambersburg PA
CBHW031609040426

42452CB00006B/455